LET'S BATTLE

COUPLES EDITION

First English edition
September 2025.

There's one thing you've probably always wanted to know.
Which one of you is actually better?

Who has more brains, faster hands, and better nerves?
This Advent calendar will reveal it – relentlessly, day after day.
It is your **daily head-to-head duel.**
No excuses, no sugarcoating:
Behind every door lurks a new challenge.
Sometimes a puzzle, sometimes a game, sometimes pure thrills.
And the rule is always: only those who are faster, smarter, or more skilled will earn points.

You have 24 days to prove it to the other person.
And in the end? It will be clear in black and white who came out on top during Advent –
and who didn't.
So come on, you two: show who's really in charge.
Advent is not a time for cuddling – Advent is a duel.

So, here's how it works:

The course of a day

Open the door → Sit opposite each other. Open the page with the number corresponding to the day.

Read the instructions → One person reads the instructions for today's game aloud.

Prepare → Have a pen and scissors ready, and set the timer or cell phone stopwatch.

Start signal → Count down together – 3, 2, 1 – go!

Turn the page & play → Both players solve the task on their page as quickly as possible or play against each other.

Award points → The first player to finish correctly wins and gets the points.
- In case of a tie: both players get the point.
- In case of mistakes: only the player with the correct solution gets the point.

Record the interim score → enter your points on the next page.

Final → On December 24, the scores will be tallied – whoever has the most points is the Advent champion!🏆

Here are the competitors: .... VS ....

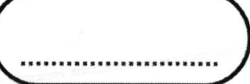

	Points:			Points:	
December 1			December 13		
December 2			December 14		
December 3			December 15		
December 4			December 16		
December 5			December 17		
December 6			December 18		
December 7			December 19		
December 8			December 20		
December 9			December 21		
December 10			December 22		
December 11			December 23		
December 12			December 24		

Certificate

ADVENT CHAMPION

goes to:

____

Whether with brains, quick hands, or just plain luck—you have defeated your opponent and claimed victory.
But beware: the title is only valid until next Advent!
Then it's time to sharpen your pencils,
set the timer, and get ready for another duel!

Rudolf

1

City. Country. Christmas.

Game material:

One pen for each player.

Here's how it works:

Both players get the same categories. One player says "A" out loud and then continues counting in their head: A, B, C ... The other player calls out "Stop!" at some point. The letter that is stopped at is the game letter for that round.
Now both players have to find a suitable word with this letter in each category as quickly as possible. So, you need to find one city, one country and something related to Christmas starting with the letter.
Example: Letter W → "Washington, Wales, 'We wish you a Merry Christmas.'"

Award yourselves points:

- Your own unique word = 2 points
- Both have the same word = 1 point
- No word = 0 points

Scoring:
After 4 rounds, the player with the most points wins. They receive 2 winner points. Enter them at the top of the overview!

Player 1

City. Country. Christmas.

CITY	COUNTRY	HOLIDAY TUNE	GIFT IDEA	COOKIE SELECTION	WINTER BEVERAGE	POINTS

TOTAL POINTS:

Player 2

City. Country. Christmas.

CITY	COUNTRY	HOLIDAY TUNE	GIFT IDEA	COOKIE SELECTION	WINTER BEVERAGE	POINTS
					TOTAL POINTS:	

2

Duel Sudoku

Game material:

One pen for each player.

Here's how it works:

Both players solve the same Sudoku puzzle at the same time. The goal is to complete the puzzle correctly as quickly as possible.
The numbers 1 to 9 must appear exactly once in each 3x3 box, each row, and each column.

Scoring:

- The first player to submit an error-free Sudoku wins the round.
- If both players finish at the same time, the points are shared.
- The winner receives 2 victory points.
- Enter the points at the top of the overview.

Player 1

Duel Sudoku

6						5		
7	4	1	6					9
	5			2		6		
8	3	7		5		4		
				6		3		8
		6	2					
9	1	8			6			2
	6				8		5	
5				9			6	4

Player 2

Duel Sudoku

6						5		
7	4	1	6					9
	5			2		6		
8	3	7		5		4		
				6		3		8
		6	2					
9	1	8			6			2
	6				8		5	
5				9			6	4

3

Help Santa Claus: Discover the path.

Game material:

1 pen per Person

Here's how it works:

Santa Claus has lost his way! Only if he finds his way through the snowy maze in time will the presents arrive under the tree on time.
Your task: Guide him from the start to the presents as quickly as possible.

- Both players start at the same time.
- Each player draws the path through the maze with their pen.
- Note: Only correct paths count – no shortcuts through the walls!
- The first player to reach the presents shouts "Ho, ho, ho!"

Scoring:

- The fastest player wins.
- The winner receives 2 points.
- Enter the points in the overview at the front.

Player 1

Help Santa Claus: Discover the path.

Player 2

Help Santa Claus: discover the path.

4

Spot The Difference

Game material:

1 pen per Person

Here's how it works:

The Christmas elf was careless again and left two almost identical pictures while painting – but there are 6 mistakes hidden in one of them!

- Both players have the same two pictures side by side.
- Start at the same time.
- Task: Find and mark all 6 mistakes as quickly as possible.

Scoring:

- The first player to mark all mistakes correctly wins.
- The winner receives 2 points.
- Enter the points in the overview at the front.

Player 1

Spot The Difference

Player 2

Spot The Difference

5

Advent Tic-Tac-Toe

Game material:

1 pen per Person

Here's how it works:

Play not just one, but a series of 5 rounds of tic-tac-toe. The first player to win 3 rounds wins the match.
The game is played on a 3x3 grid.
One player is ✕ the other is ◯.
Take turns placing your symbols on the board.
Three identical symbols in a row (horizontal, vertical, or diagonal) = win the round.

Scoring:

- The first player to win 3 rounds is the overall winner.
- The winner receives 2 points.
- Enter the points in the overview at the front.

Advent Tiv–Tac–Toe

○ you compete directly against one another

Winner:

Winner:

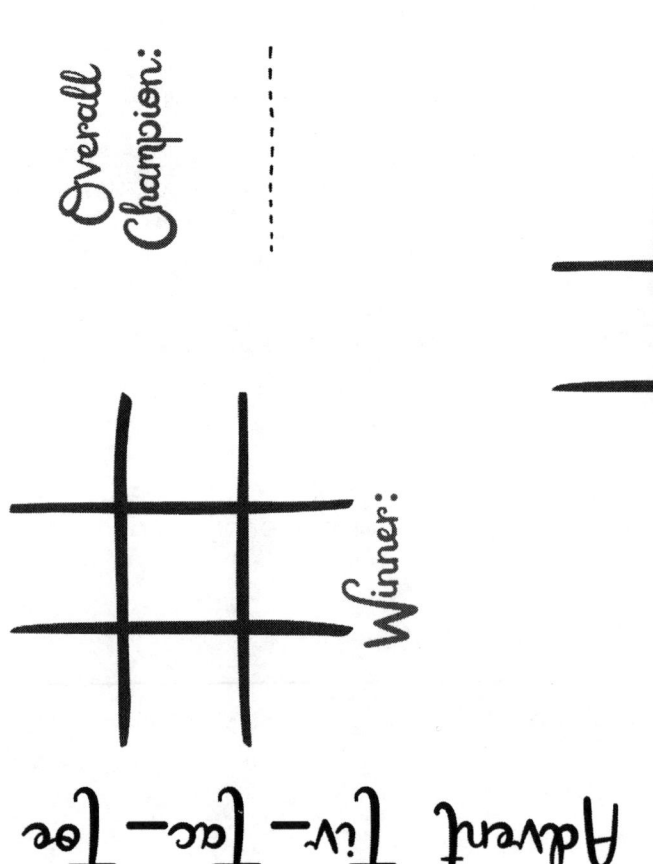

Overall Champion:

✕ you compete directly against one another

Advent Tiv_Tac_Toe

Winner:

Winner:

Winner:

6.

Crack the code

Game material:

1 pen per Person

Here's how it works:

In this crossword puzzle, the terms are represented by small pictures rather than questions. Each picture stands for a solution word that must be entered in the appropriate box.
Both players have the same puzzle.
Solve the pictures and enter the words in the crossword puzzle.
Some boxes contain small numbers – the letters in these boxes together form the solution word.
The first player to recognize the solution word calls "Stop!".

Scoring:

- If the player has the correct solution word, they win the round immediately.
- The winner receives 2 points.
- Enter the points at the top of the overview.

Player 1

Crack the code

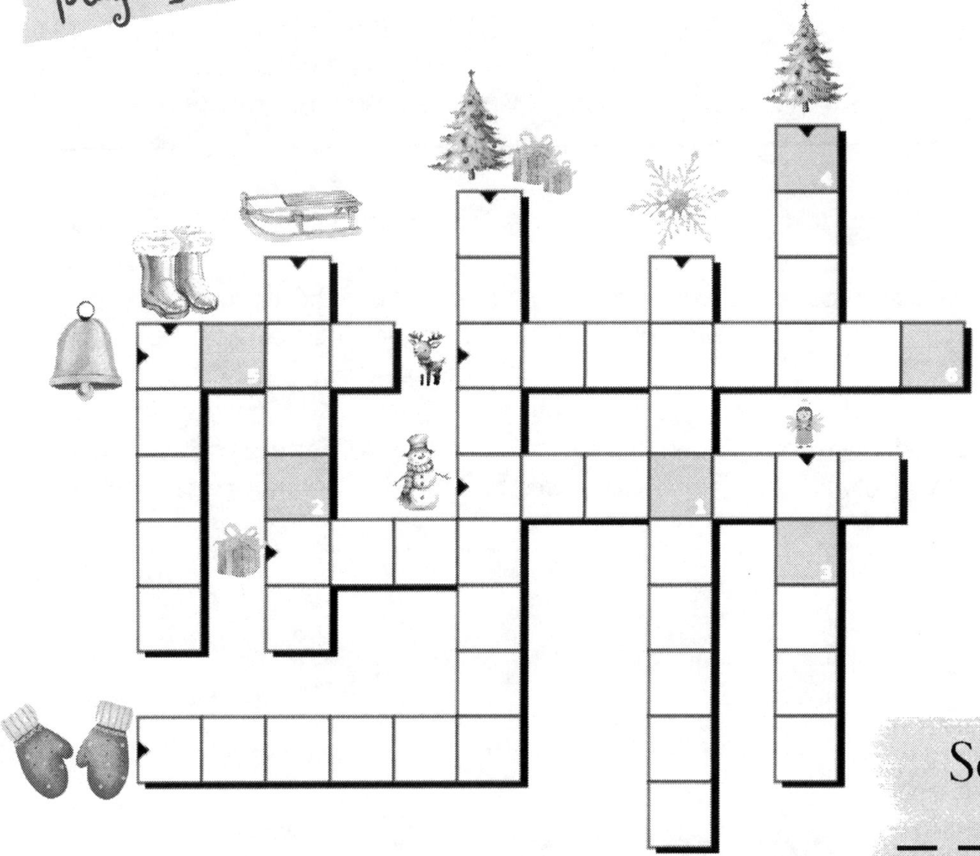

Solution:

__ __ __ __ __ __

1 2 3 4 5 6

Player 2

Crack the code

Solution:

_ _ _ _ _ _

1 2 3 4 5 6

7

Battlegift

Game material:

1 pen per person
1 large book (or similar) to create a screen between you

Here's how it works:

The players hunt for their opponents' hidden Christmas presents. Each player has a 10x10 grid on which they secretly mark their presents. Then they take turns guessing where the presents are hidden.

- Each player takes turns calling out a coordinate (e.g., "B7").
- If they hit an opponent's gift there, the opponent says "Hit!".
- If an entire pile of gifts is sunk, the opponent says "Pile of gifts sunk!".
- The goal is to find and sink all of your opponent's piles of gifts.

Scoring:

- The first player to sink all of their opponent's gifts wins.
- The winner receives 2 points.
- Enter the points in the overview at the front.

Player 1

Battlegift

my gifts

	1	2	3	4	5	6	7	8	9	
A	10									
B										
C										
D										
E										
F										
G										
H										
I										
J										

gifts from enemy

	1	2	3	4	5	6	7	8	9	
A	10									
B										
C										
D										
E										
F										
G										
H										
I										
J										

4x

3x

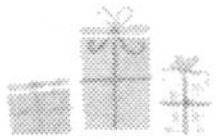

2x

1x

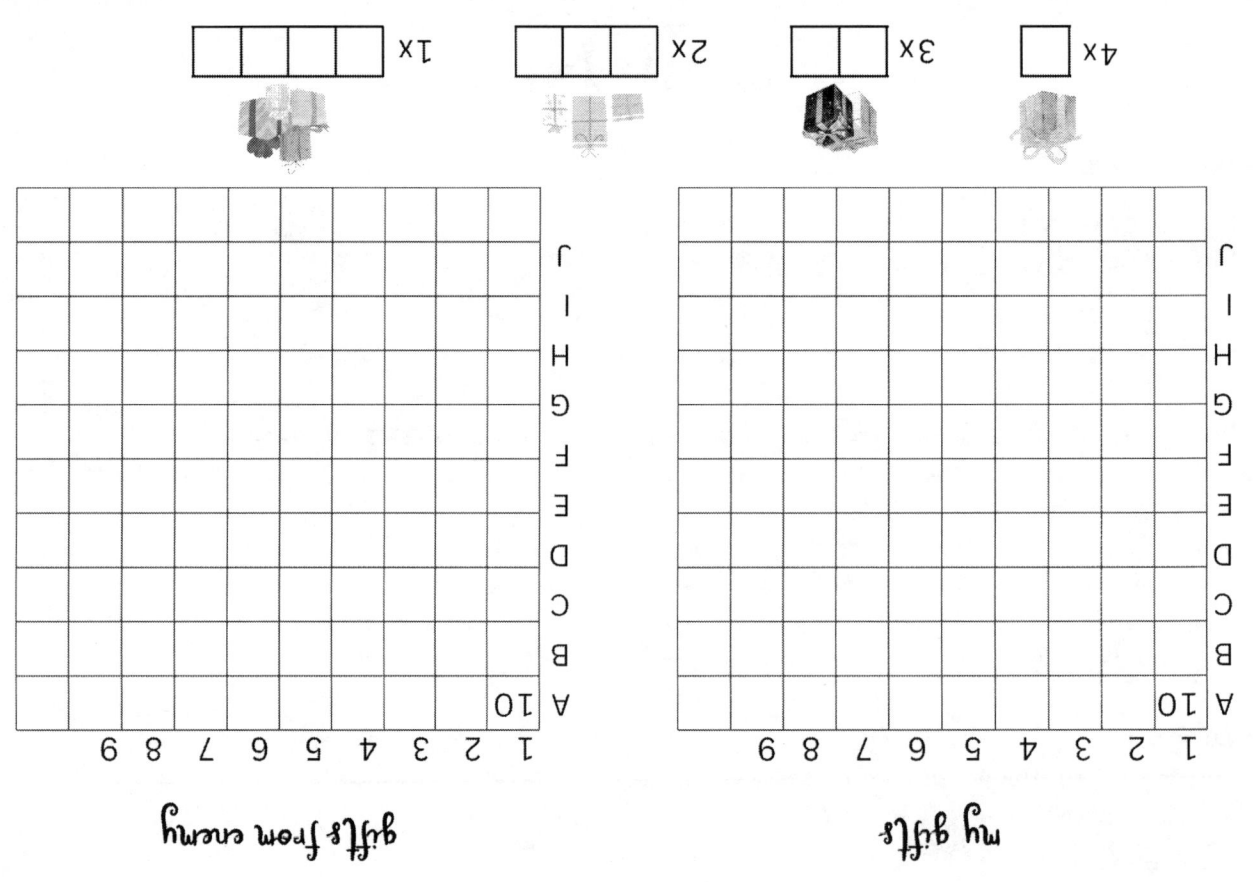

Player 2

Battlegift

my gifts

	1	2	3	4	5	6	7	8	9	10
A										
B										
C										
D										
E										
F										
G										
H										
I										
J										

gifts from enemy

	1	2	3	4	5	6	7	8	9	10
A										
B										
C										
D										
E										
F										
G										
H										
I										
J										

4x

3x

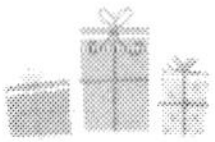

2x

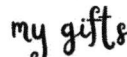

1x

8

Pile of gifts

Game material:

1 pen per Person

Here's how it works:

The number pyramid is structured like a small mountain of gifts: each number at the top is the sum of the two numbers below it.
Your task: fill in the empty fields with the correct numbers as quickly as possible until the mountain is complete.

- Both players start at the same time.
- Each number = sum of the two fields directly below it.
- The first player to correctly complete the gift mountains calls out "Done!".

Scoring:

- The fastest player with the correct solution wins.
- If there are any mistakes, the solution does not count.
- The winner receives 2 points.
- Enter the points in the overview at the front.

Player 1

Pile of gifts

30			
	17		
6			
	0		

50				
		27		
	11		16	
	8			

Player 2

Pile of gifts

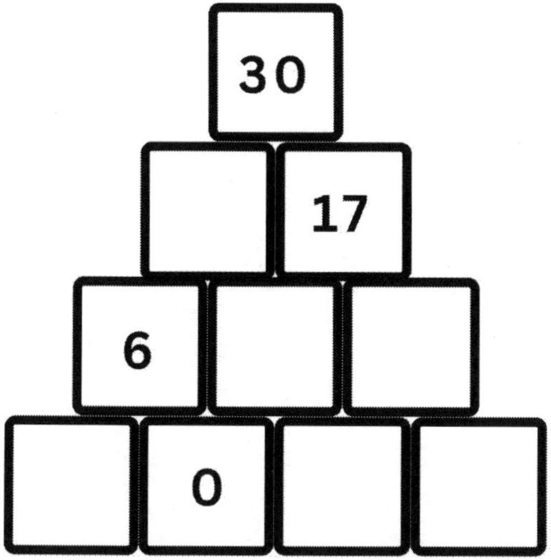

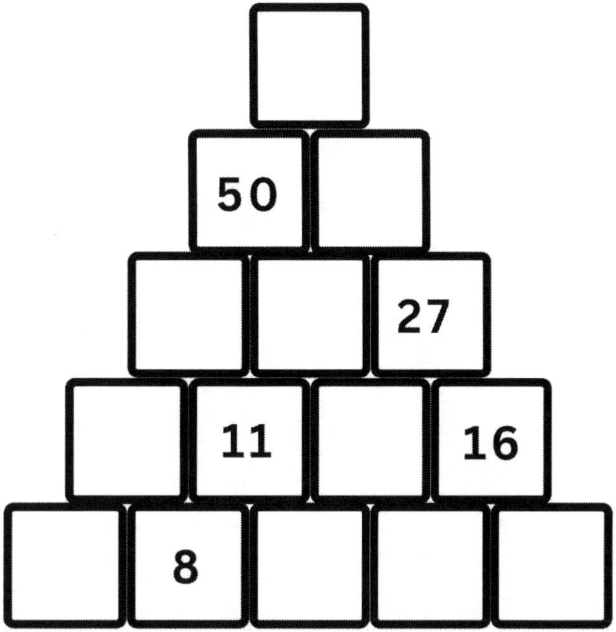

9.

The paper airplane contest

Game material:

One pair of scissors for each person.

Here's how it works:

Today, there's no calculating or puzzling – it's time to fly!
Cut out your page at the marked spot and use it to make a paper airplane.

The first person to finish calls "Stop!" and gets the first victory point.
The other player is allowed to finish making their paper airplane.

Then you compete against each other: each player throws their airplane once.
The plane that flies farther wins the second victory point.

Important note:
This page with the instructions and the page with the number 10 are cut out during crafting. Make sure to continue at the right place in the Advent calendar the next day!

And now: 3 - 2 - 1 - go!

Player 1

The paper airplane contest

Player 2

The paper airplane contest

10

Dots and Boxes Showdown

Game material:

One pen for each person in various colors.

Here's how it works:

The playing field consists of many dots. Take turns drawing a line between two adjacent dots (horizontally or vertically).
If a player closes a box with their line, they may draw a cross in the box in their color—and immediately take another turn.

- The goal is to capture as many boxes as possible.
- The game is played until all lines have been drawn.
- At the end, the marked squares are counted.

On one side you will find the first game.
On the opposite side is the rematch.

Scoring:

- Each game won is worth 1 point.
- Enter the points in the overview at the front.

Game 1

Dots and Boxes Showdown

Revenge

Dots and Boxes Showdown

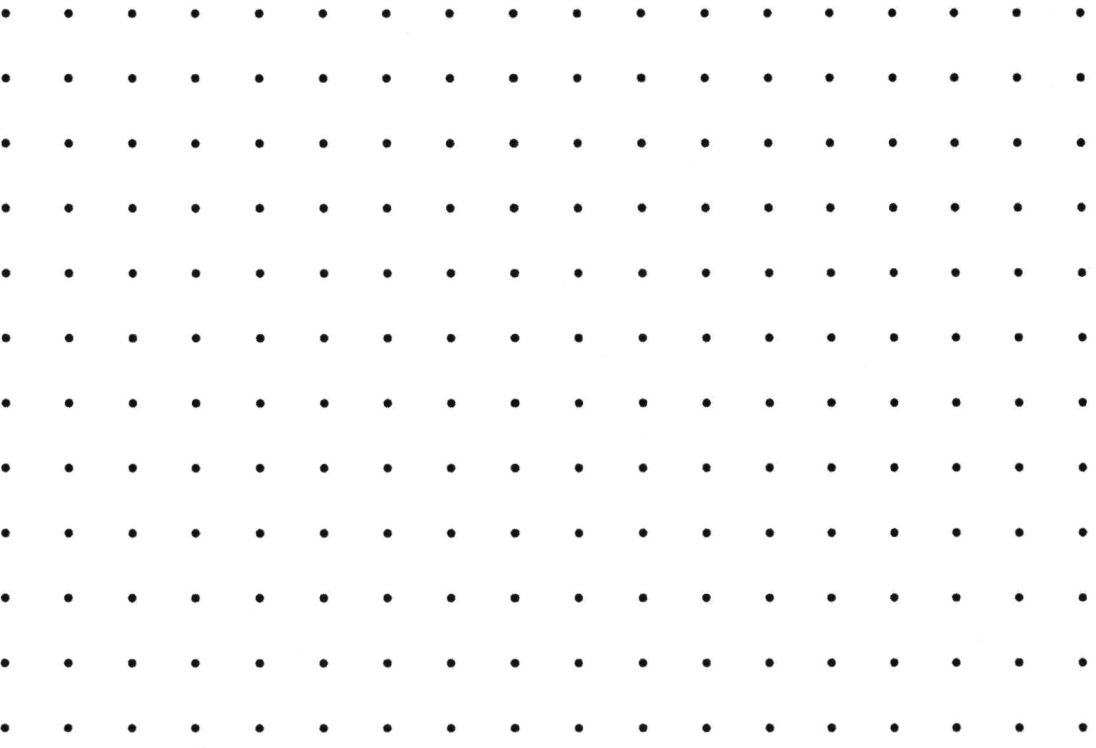

11

Christmas word chain

Game material:

1 Pen per Person
1 stopwatch

Here's how it works:

You have 3 minutes to form the longest possible chain of words.

- Set your stopwatch to 3 minutes.
- Start with the given word (Example: Santa).
- The next word has to be another word that starts with the last letter of the previous word. (Example: Santa → Angel →lights---).
- Write down the word chain.
- You can't repeat words that has already been used

Scoring:

- After 3 minutes, count your words.
- Each correct word is worth 1 point.
- Each Christmas-related word is worth 2 points.
- The player with the most points wins the round.
- The winner receives 2 winner points.
- Enter the points in the overview at the front.

Player 1

Christmas word chain

TOTAL POINTS:

Player 2

Christmas word chain

TOTAL POINTS:

12

Indoor Olympics

Game material:

Just you.

Here's how it works:

Today's motto is: Get up and move! In the Indoor Olympics, each player receives a list of fun mini-tasks. Both players have the same tasks, but in different order.

- At your joint signal, both players start at the same time and turn to the next page.
- Each player works through their tasks one after the other.
- The tasks require movement – so you have to get up from your seat!

Scoring:

- The first player to complete their last task calls out "Stop!" loudly.
- This player wins the round.
- The winner receives 2 winner points.
- Enter the points at the top of the overview.

Player 1

Indoor Olympics

- [ ] **Snowflake spen:** Spen around 5 times and land with your arms outstretched like a snowflake.
- [ ] **Reindeer jump**: Jump around the room three times while shouting "Ho, ho, ho!"
- [ ] **Tree decoration hunt**: Fetch a Christmas decoration (e.g., bauble, star, or tinsel) and bring it back.
- [ ] **Sprint**: Run as fast as you can to the bathroom and back.
- [ ] **Christmas carol flash**: Sing a line from a Christmas carol immediately.
- [ ] **Cookie run**: Get something edible from the kitchen and come back.
- [ ] **Winter style**: Put on a hat, scarf, and gloves and shout "Ready!"

Player 2

Indoor Olympics

- [ ] **Snowflake spen:** Spen around 5 times and land with your arms outstretched like a snowflake.
- [ ] **Reindeer jump**: Jump around the room three times while shouting "Ho, ho, ho!"
- [ ] **Tree decoration hunt**: Fetch a Christmas decoration (e.g., bauble, star, or tinsel) and bring it back.
- [ ] **Sprint**: Run as fast as you can to the bathroom and back.
- [ ] **Christmas carol flash**: Sing a line from a Christmas carol immediately.
- [ ] **Cookie run**: Get something edible from the kitchen and come back.
- [ ] **Winter style**: Put on a hat, scarf, and gloves and shout "Ready!"

13

Christmas ABC

Game material:

1 pen per Person

Here's how it works:

Each player must find a Christmas-related term for each letter.

- Both players start at the same time.
- The first player to fill in all the boxes calls out "Done!".
- The terms are then checked to see which ones are valid.

Scoring:

- Each valid term is worth 1 point.
- An extra point can be awarded for particularly original words.
- The player with the most points wins the round.
- The winner receives 2 winner points.
- Enter the points in the overview at the front.

Player 2

Christmas ABC

A	J	S
B	K	T
C	L	U
D	M	V
E	N	W
F	O	X
G	P	Y
H	Q	Z
I	R	POINTS: ------------

Player 2

Christmas ABC

A	J	S
B	K	T
C	L	U
D	M	V
E	N	W
F	O	X
G	P	Y
H	Q	Z
I	R	POINTS: ----------

14

Mirror, mirror on the wall.

Game material:

1 pen per Person

Here's how it works:

Each player receives half of a template. Your task is to trace the missing second half as accurately as possible in mirror image.

- Both players start at the same time.
- The first player to completely mirror the template calls "Done!" and receives the first point.
- Then the two players compare their work: the player who has created the most accurate and cleanest mirror image receives the second point.

Scoring:

- A maximum of 2 points per round is possible (one for speed, one for accuracy).
- Enter the points in the overview at the front.

Player 1

Mirror, mirror on the wall.

Player 2

Mirror, mirror on the wall.

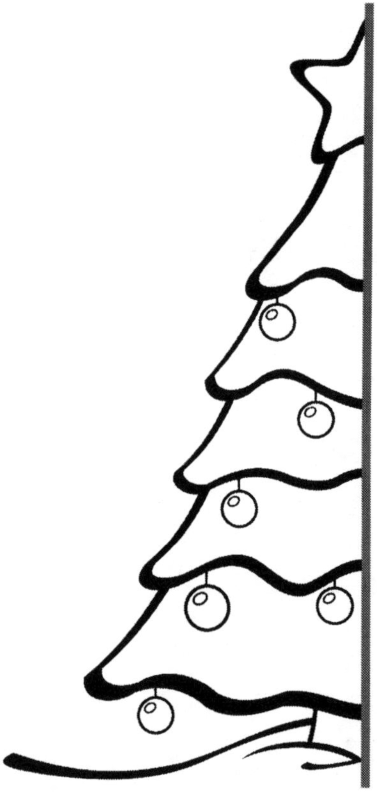

15

Christmas word hunt

Game material:

1 pen per Person

Here's how it works:

Eight Christmas-themed words are hidden in a grid of letters. The words can be found horizontally, vertically, diagonally, and even backwards in the grid.

- Both players have the same search grid.
- Start at the same time.
- Find all 8 hidden words and mark them with the pen.

Scoring:

- The first player to find and mark all 8 words correctly wins the round.
- The winner receives 2 points.
- Enter the points in the overview at the front.

Player 1

Christmas word hunt

M	E	A	T	S	L	E	I	G	H	T	I	P	W	P	S	H	S	H	X
G	K	L	D	A	I	L	T	U	L	C	V	K	S	K	T	Q	H	C	Q
Q	R	Z	X	F	S	O	I	V	H	I	T	O	G	A	A	K	E	K	G
K	N	C	R	N	D	D	K	G	J	U	U	K	J	A	R	O	F	F	S
S	Z	N	V	G	M	T	M	U	K	P	L	C	A	N	D	L	E	S	M
D	I	I	P	E	W	A	I	R	S	A	O	H	Z	D	C	M	O	C	S
F	W	Y	R	B	J	S	T	A	R	D	U	S	T	Y	I	D	N	C	O
B	S	B	S	E	B	P	B	R	Y	K	N	J	Z	M	G	H	F	G	N
Q	K	H	T	B	F	C	U	V	U	J	T	V	G	L	I	W	Q	U	G
C	J	S	E	E	I	B	L	R	T	P	W	A	T	Y	S	Y	U	C	I
C	H	R	I	S	T	M	A	S	Z	T	Q	C	I	A	P	U	A	T	S
U	F	A	T	W	I	M	T	M	W	E	E	O	G	L	R	H	Z	S	B
U	W	A	K	J	N	M	F	H	G	G	P	O	E	I	I	J	O	S	G
V	N	P	I	X	M	J	B	G	G	C	H	K	K	C	N	F	R	A	Z
S	I	I	I	O	E	M	F	H	X	R	P	I	Q	H	K	K	Y	S	B
F	X	B	K	B	A	T	U	B	I	G	R	E	O	W	L	E	S	S	E
E	H	F	Y	M	Z	S	R	Y	K	T	J	S	W	H	E	B	I	R	R
G	I	F	T	S	L	C	E	D	P	V	X	L	F	J	S	P	O	M	Y
Q	W	Q	L	M	G	E	Z	U	C	R	P	R	Y	H	P	S	X	I	S
V	R	E	I	N	D	E	E	R	N	S	O	R	E	D	J	C	X	A	D

COOKIES
GIFTS
REINDEER
STARDUST
CANDLES
SLED
SPRINKLES
CHRISTMAS TREE
STAR

Player 2

Christmas word hunt

M	E	A	T	S	L	E	I	G	H	T	I	P	W	P	S	H	S	H	X
G	K	L	D	A	I	L	T	U	L	C	V	K	S	K	T	Q	H	C	Q
Q	R	Z	X	F	S	O	I	V	H	I	T	O	G	A	A	K	E	K	G
K	N	C	R	N	D	D	K	G	J	U	U	K	J	A	R	O	F	F	S
S	Z	N	V	G	M	T	M	U	K	P	L	C	A	N	D	L	E	S	M
D	I	I	P	E	W	A	I	R	S	A	O	H	Z	D	C	M	O	C	S
F	W	Y	R	B	J	S	T	A	R	D	U	S	T	Y	I	D	N	C	O
B	S	B	S	E	B	P	B	R	Y	K	N	J	Z	M	G	H	F	G	N
Q	K	H	T	B	F	C	U	V	U	J	T	V	G	L	I	W	Q	U	G
C	J	S	E	E	I	B	L	R	T	P	W	A	T	Y	S	Y	U	C	I
C	H	R	I	S	T	M	A	S	Z	T	Q	C	I	A	P	U	A	T	S
U	F	A	T	W	I	M	T	M	W	E	E	O	G	L	R	H	Z	S	B
U	W	A	K	J	N	M	F	H	G	G	P	O	E	I	I	J	O	S	G
V	N	P	I	X	M	J	B	G	G	C	H	K	K	C	N	F	R	A	Z
S	I	I	I	O	E	M	F	H	X	R	P	I	Q	H	K	K	Y	S	B
F	X	B	K	B	A	T	U	B	I	G	R	E	O	W	L	E	S	S	E
E	H	F	Y	M	Z	S	R	Y	K	T	J	S	W	H	E	B	I	R	R
G	I	F	T	S	L	C	E	D	P	V	X	L	F	J	S	P	O	M	Y
Q	W	Q	L	M	G	E	Z	U	C	R	P	R	Y	H	P	S	X	I	S
V	R	E	I	N	D	E	E	R	N	S	O	R	E	D	J	C	X	A	D

COOKIES
GIFTS
REINDEER
STARDUST
CANDLES
SLED
SPRINKLES
CHRISTMAS TREE
STAR

16

Footprints in the snow

Game material:

1 pen per person
Something straight per person (ruler or similar)

Here's how it works:

On the page, you will see several symbols distributed on the left and right. Your task is to connect the matching pairs with a line.
When all symbols are correctly connected, the marked letters from top to bottom form a solution word.

- Both players start at the same time.
- Connect the symbols correctly and write down the solution word.
- The first player to find the solution word calls "Stop!".
- This player may now look at the solutions.

Scoring:

- If the solution word is correct, the player wins and receives 2 points.
- If the solution word is incorrect, the opponent receives 2 points.
- Enter the points in the overview at the front.

Attention: Now turn the book 90 degrees and then: 3 - 2 - 1 - GO!!

Player 1

Footprints in the snow

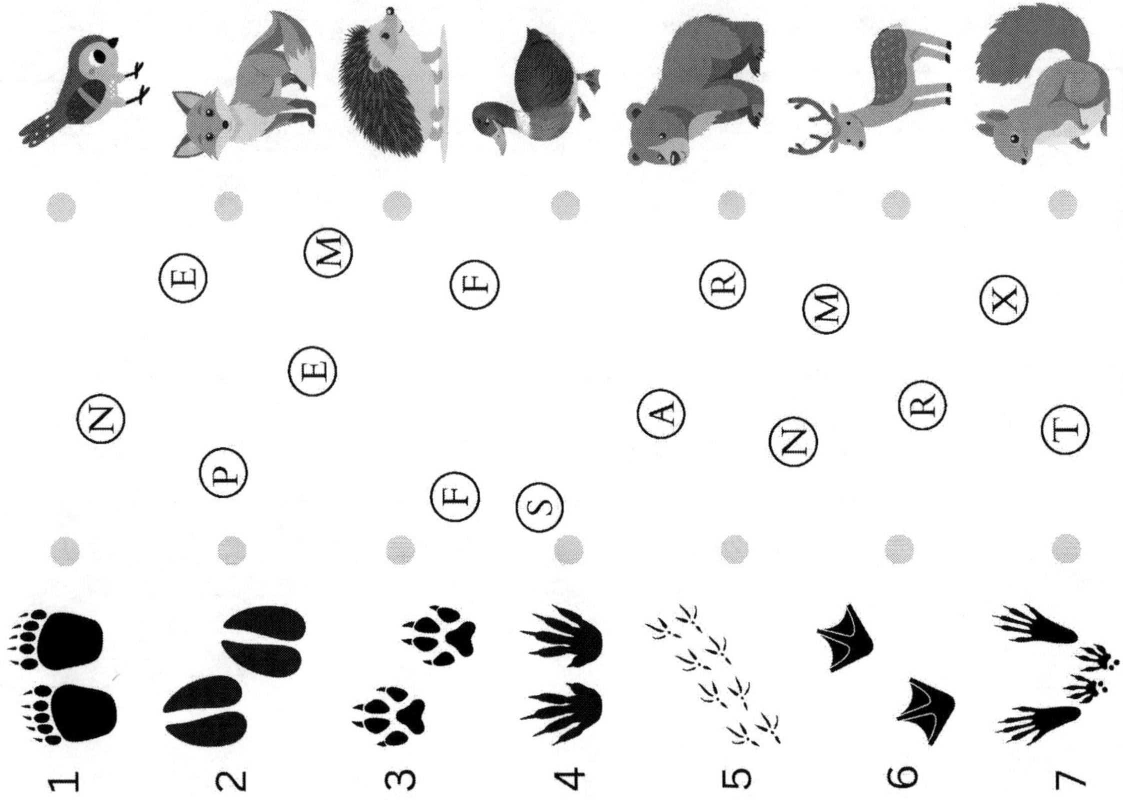

Solution: _ _ _ _ _ _ _

Player 2

Footprints in the snow

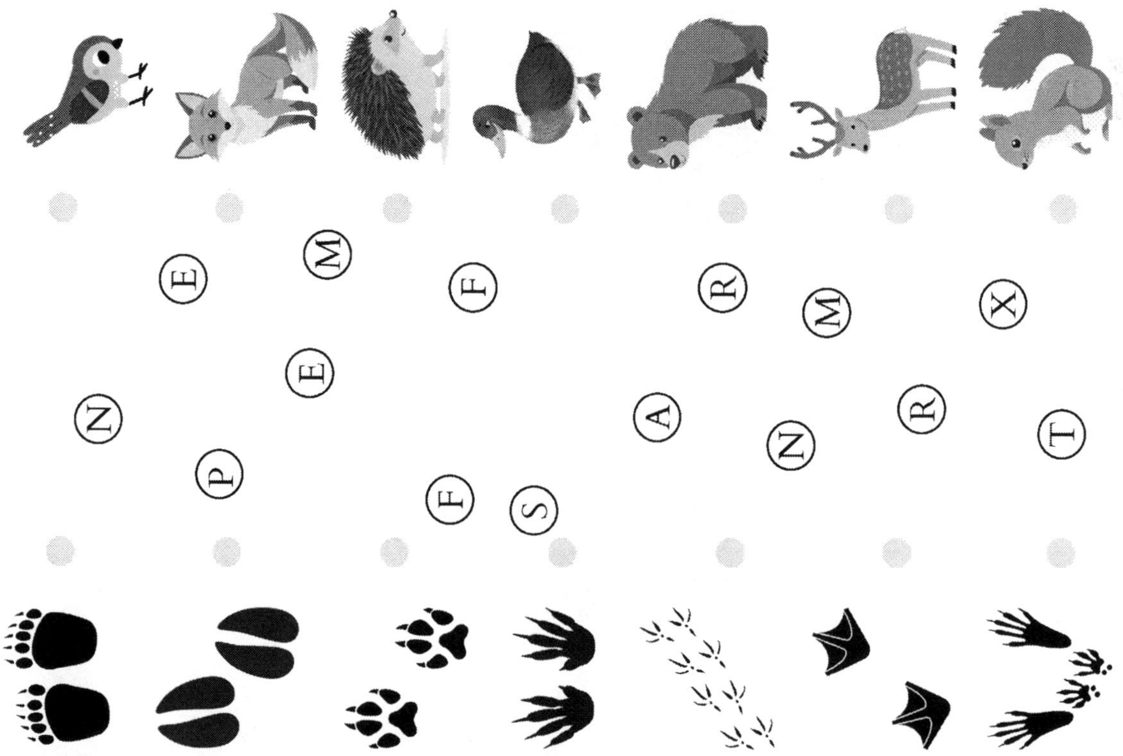

Solution: _ _ _ _ _ _ _

17

Christmas Elf Trails

Game material:

1 pen per Person

Here's how it works:

The Christmas elves have prepared secret paths in the snow-covered forest. Letters are scattered along these paths. Your task is to find the right paths and collect all the letters along the way.

- Start at the same time.
- Follow the right paths and collect the letters along the way.
- Enter the collected letters in the boxes at the bottom.
- At the end, these will form words.
- Whoever has entered the correct solution words calls out “Done!”.

Scoring:

- If the solution words are correct, they receive 2 points.
- If a word is incorrect, the opponent receives the 2 points.
- Enter the points in the overview at the front.

Christmas Elf Trails

Player 1

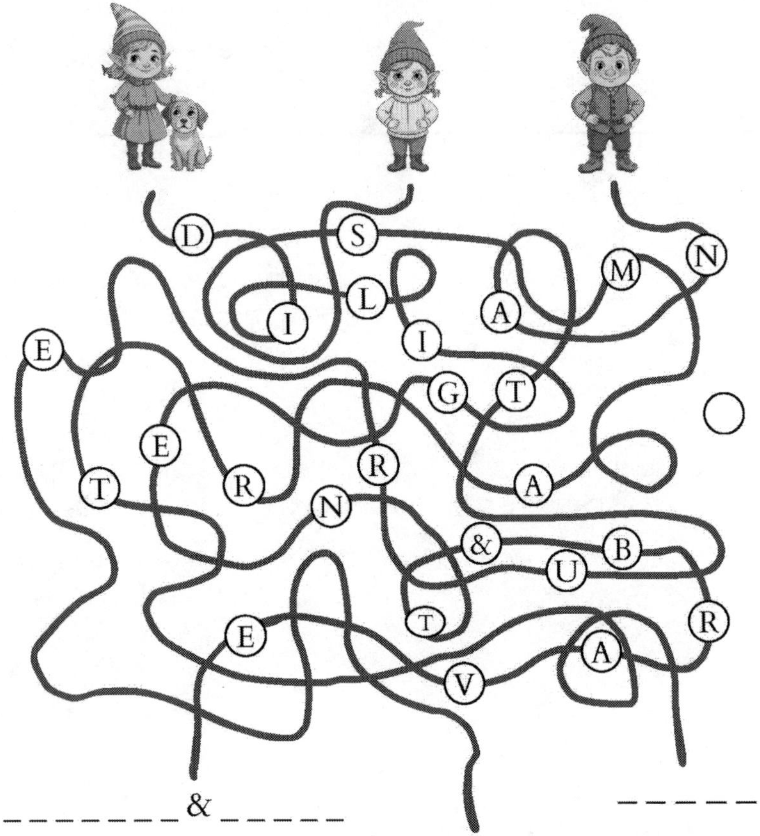

Player 2

Christmas Elf Trails

_ _ _ _ _ _ _ _ & _ _ _ _ _   _ _ _ _ _

_ _ _ _ _

18

Quick _ drawer

Game material:

1 pen per Person

Here's how it works:

Today, speed and creativity count! Each player is given the same drawing task.

- Both start at the same time.
- The goal: to finish as quickly as possible while still creating a beautiful picture.

Scoring:

- The player who finishes first receives 1 point.
- The player with the best picture (decided jointly or by a neutral person) also receives 1 point.
- Enter the points in the overview at the front.

Player 1

Quick_drawer

Draw Santa Claus with a hat and a sack on his sleigh!

Player 2

Quick_drawer

Draw Santa Claus with a hat and a sack on his sleigh!

19

Emoji riddle

Game material:

Material

Here's how it works:

On the page, you'll find a bunch of emojis.
A bunch of emojis together stands for a song.
Can you track down the perfect Christmas songs?

Once a player has figured out all the songs, they shout "Stop!"

Scoring:

- If all the songs are right, that player wins the round and gets 2 points.
- If a song is incorrect, the other player receives 2 points.
- Please input the points at the beginning of the overview.

Player 1

Emoji riddle

1. 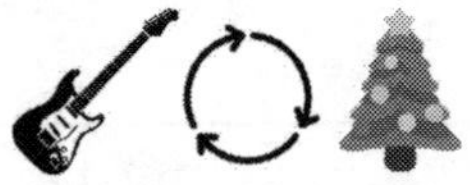

2. 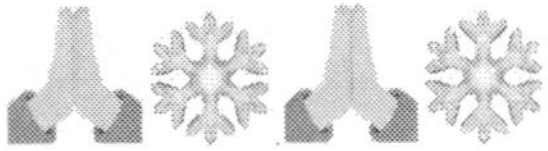

3. 

4. 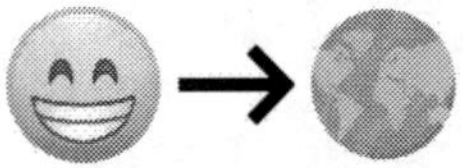

5. 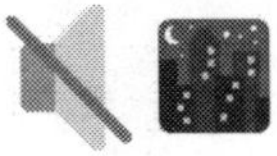

6. 

Player 2

Emoji riddle

1.  ....

2.  ....

3. 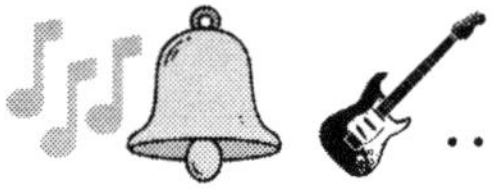 ....

4. 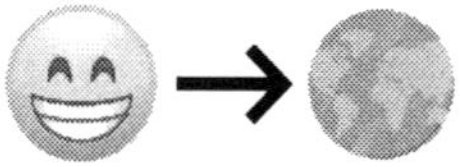 ....

5. 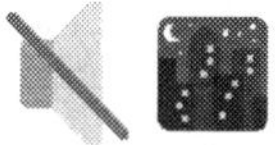 ....

6.  ....

20

Connect Four

Game material:

1 pen per Person

Here's how it works:

Play the classic game of Connect Four on your paper board. The aim is to be the first to place four of your symbols in a row – horizontally, vertically, or diagonally.

How to play:
One player plays with X, the other with O.
Take turns “dropping” a piece into a column (on paper: mark the next free space in that column starting from the bottom).
The first player to get four in a row wins the game.

Scoring:

- Each game won is worth 1 point.
- Enter the points in the overview at the front.

Game 1

Connect Four

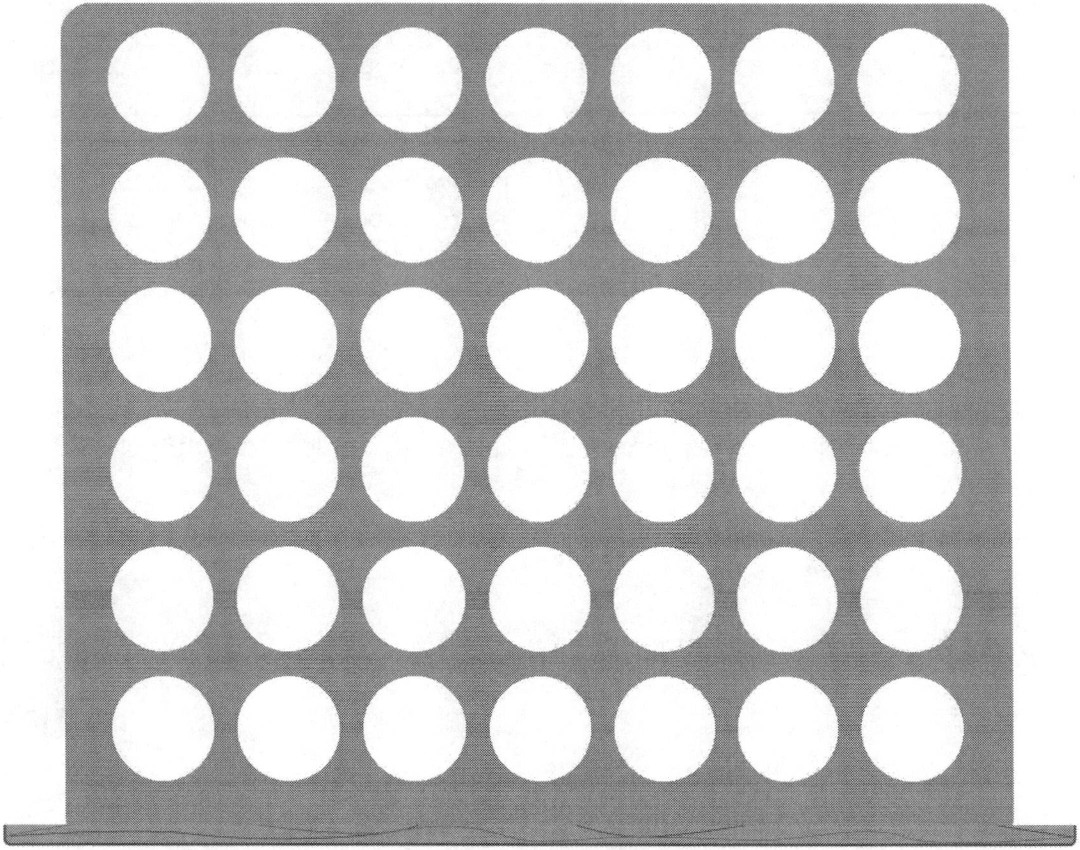

Revenge

Connect Four

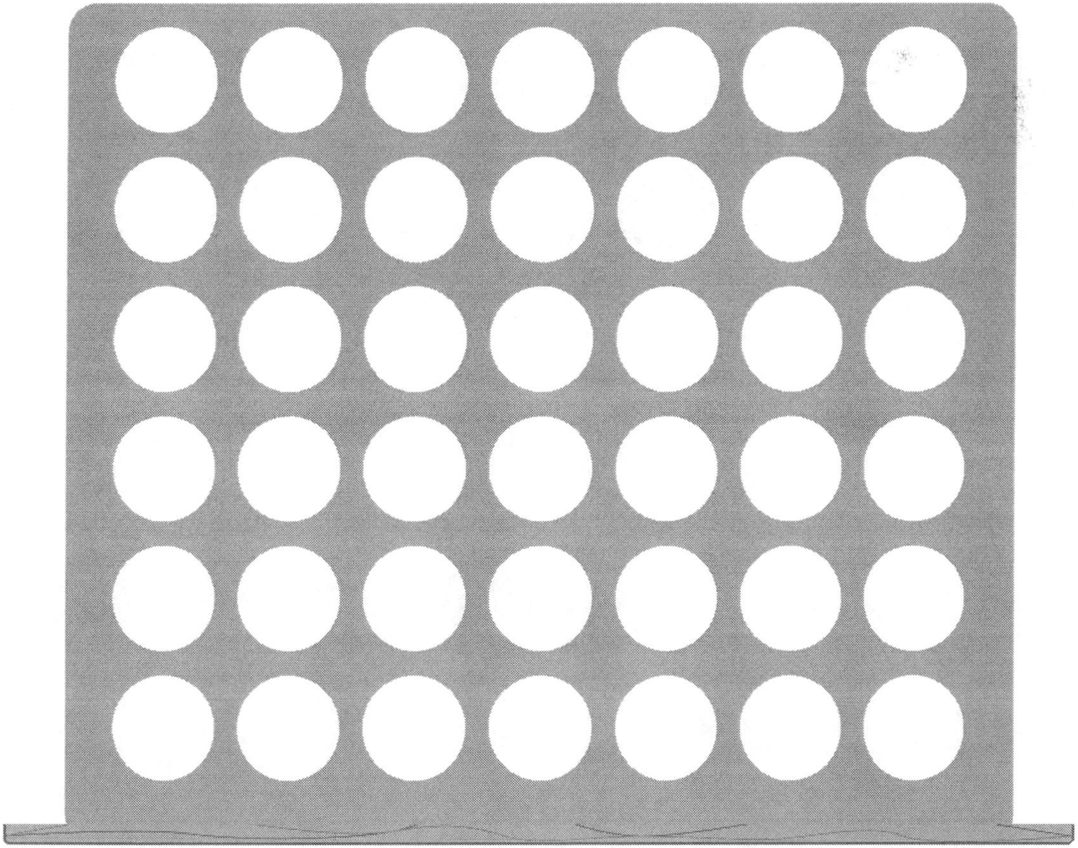

21

Who am I ?

Game material:

1 pen per Person

Here's how it works:

Both players think of a character or person for the other player and write it down secretly on their side.

Then they take turns:
Player A asks a yes/no question about their character.
Then it's Player B's turn to ask a question.
After each question is asked, a ❄ snowflake is crossed out – this helps you keep track of the number of questions. The player who guesses their character with fewer questions wins.

Scoring:

- Each player may ask questions until they think they know the character.
- If the answer is correct, the round ends.
- If it is incorrect, 2 ❄ ❄ snowflakes are crossed out.
- Now compare who needed fewer questions – that player wins.
- The winner receives 2 points.
- Enter the points in the overview at the front.

Player 1

Who am I ?

How many questions do you need?

Figure / Person for Player 2:

Player 2

Who am I ?

How many questions do you need?

Figure / Person for Player 1:

22

Say hello to the reindeer nose!

Game material:

one pair of scissors

Here's how it works:

Today we're going to aim and flick!

- On the next page, you will find marked fields: Cut out the page, fold it in half, and form it into paper balls.
- On the following page, you will find the target.
- Together, decide on a distance from which you want to flick.

- How to play:
- Each player takes turns flicking a paper ball toward the target.
- Make sure your fingers stay behind the designated line.

Scoring:

- The player whose paper ball lands closest to the center of the target wins.
- The winner receives 2 points.
- Enter the points in the overview at the front.

Player 1

Player 2

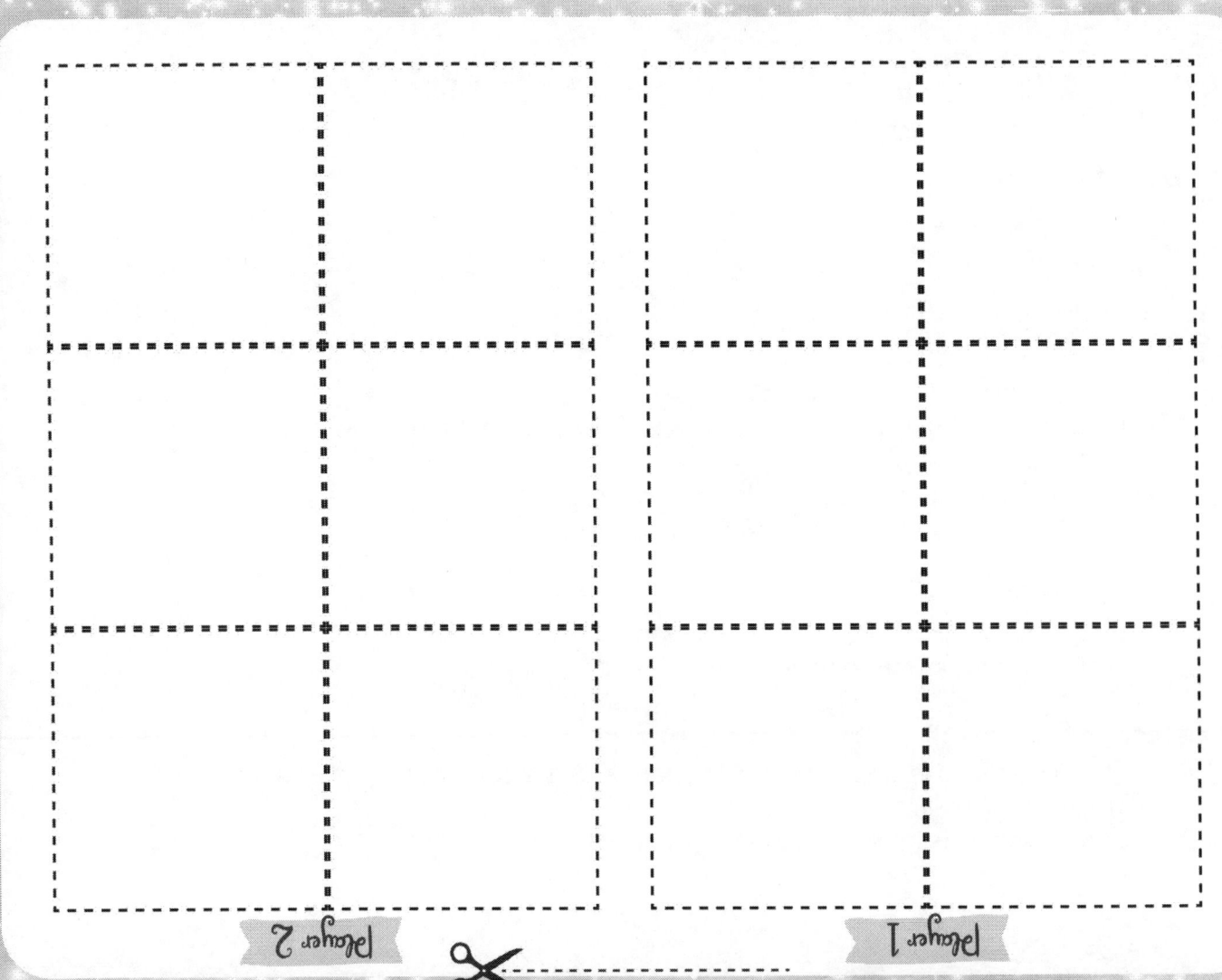

Say hello to the reindeer nose!

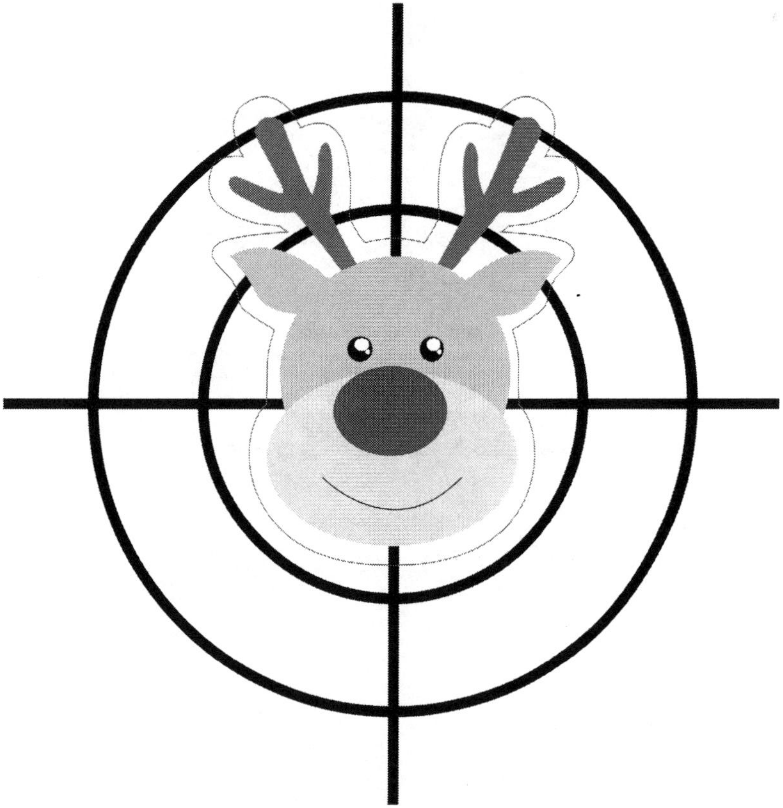

23

Tower to the North Pole

Game material:

check the next page (later!)

Here's how it works:

On the next page, you will find a list of items that are the same for both players. Both players must first collect all of the items listed as quickly as possible. Once you have all of the items, you can start building.
Use all of the items you have collected to build a tower.

Important: You must use all of the items!
As soon as a player is finished, he must shout "Stop!"

Scoring:

- The player who finishes first receives 1 point.
- The player with the taller tower also receives 1 point.
- This means there are a total of 2 points to be earned.
- Enter the points in the overview at the front.

Player 1

North Pole Tower

collect:

1 book

1 remote control

1 shoe

1 Food

1 toilet paper roll

1 bottle

Player 2

North Pole Tower

collect:

1 book

1 remote control

1 shoe

1 Food

1 toilet paper roll

1 bottle

24

Christmas puzzle

Game material:

One pair of scissors for each person.

Here's how it works:

Today's task: grab your scissors and get started! On this page, you will find a Christmas picture that you must first cut out. Then, put the pieces back together as quickly as possible.
The first person to finish calls out "Stop!" loudly.

Scoring:

- The player who is the first to complete the puzzle correctly wins the round and receives 2 points.
- Enter the points in the overview at the front.

Player 1

Player 2

Solutions

2

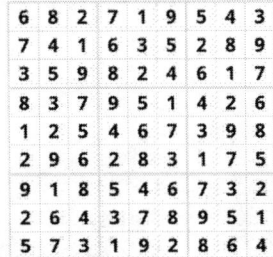

6	8	2	7	1	9	5	4	3
7	4	1	6	3	5	2	8	9
3	5	9	8	2	4	6	1	7
8	3	7	9	5	1	4	2	6
1	2	5	4	6	7	3	9	8
2	9	6	2	8	3	1	7	5
9	1	8	5	4	6	7	3	2
2	6	4	3	7	8	9	5	1
5	7	3	1	9	2	8	6	4

3

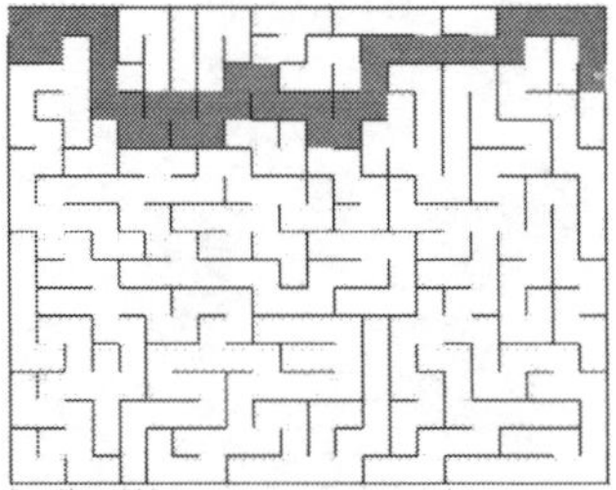

4

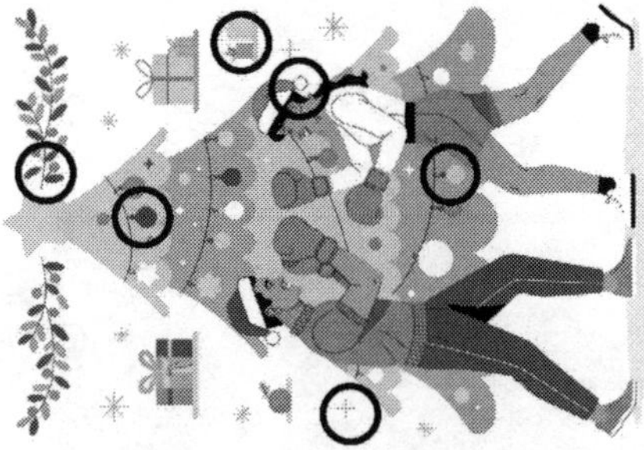

6

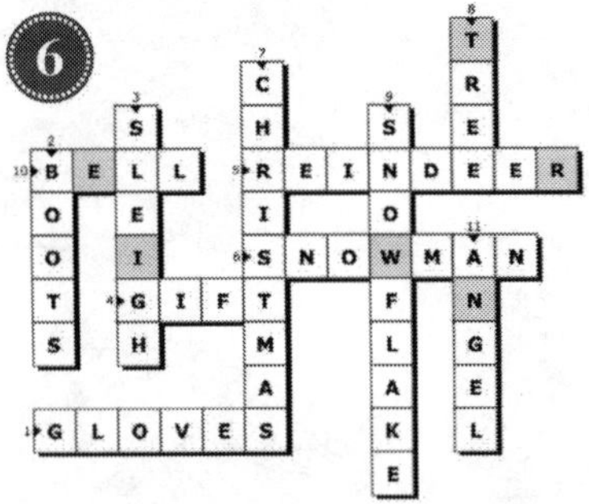

8

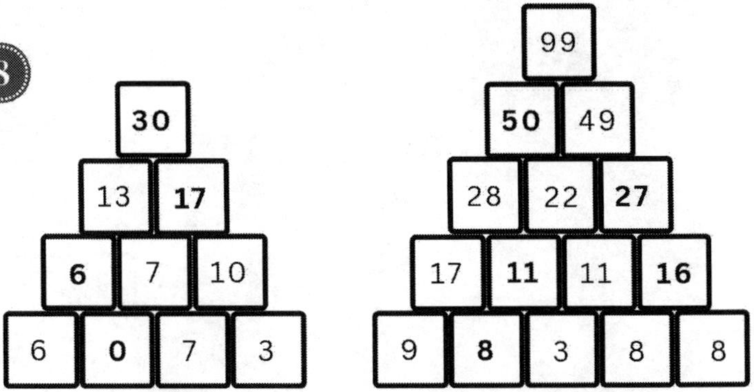

15

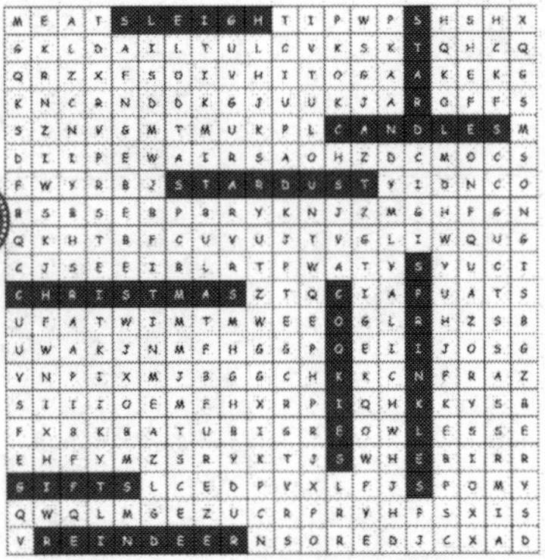

16

Solution:
Present

17

19

1. Rockin' around the Christmas tree
2. Let it snow, let it snow
3. Jingle bell rock
4. Joy to the world
5. Silent night
6. I'm dreaming of a white christmas

Imprint

English-language first edition September 2025.

Lilly Schoen is represented by:
Tikva Verlag GmbH
Schillerstraße 26
79183 Waldkirch
Germany

ISBN: 978-3-911597-30-2

I welcome questions, suggestions, and feedback at:
philipp@tikva-verlag.de

Feel free to leave us a review on Amazon.

Made in the USA
Monee, IL
17 November 2025

35074752R00057